Peter Roe

The First and Second Ages

Proceedings of The Tolkien Society
Seminar 1990

Edited by Trevor Reynolds

Cover illustration *Kinslaying at Alqualondë* © Paula DiSante 1992
Typesetting @ Francesca Barbini 2020
Published under the auspices of the Peter Roe Memorial Fund, third in the series.

Contents

About the Peter Roe Memorial Fund

The Tolkien Society's seminar proceedings and other booklets are typically published under the auspices of the Peter Roe Memorial Fund, a fund in the Society's accounts that commemorates a young member who died in a traffic accident. Peter Roe, a young and very talented person joined the Society in 1979, shortly after his sixteenth birthday. He had discovered Middle-earth some time earlier, and was so inspired by it that he even developed his own system of runes, similar to the Dwarvish Angerthas, but which utilised logical sound values, matching the logical shapes of the runes. Peter was also an accomplished cartographer, and his bedroom was covered with multi-coloured maps of the journeys of the Fellowship, plans of Middle-earth, and other drawings.

Peter was also a creative writer in both poetry and prose—the subject being incorporated into his own *Dwarvish Chronicles*. He was so enthusiastic about having joined the Society that he had written a letter ordering all the available back issues, and was on his way to buy envelopes when he was hit by a speeding lorry outside his home.

Sometime later, Jonathan and Lester Simons (at that time Chairman and Membership Secretary respectively) visited Peter's parents to see his room and to look at the work on which he had spent so much care and attention in such a tragically short life. It was obvious that Peter had produced, and would have continued to produce, material of such a high standard as to make a complete booklet, with poetry, calligraphy, stories and cartography. The then committee set up a special account in honour of Peter, with the consent of his parents, which would be the source of finance for the Society's special publications. Over the years a number of members have made generous donations to the fund.

The first publication to be financed by the Peter Roe Memorial Fund was *Some Light on Middle-earth* by Edward Crawford, published in 1985. Subsequent publications have been composed from papers delivered at Tolkien Society workshops and seminars, talks from guest speakers at the Annual Dinner, and collections of the best articles from past issues of *Amon Hen*, the Society's bulletin.

Dwarvish Fragments, an unfinished tale by Peter, was printed in *Mallorn* 15 (September 1980). A standalone collection of Peter's creative endeavours is currently being prepared for publication.

The Peter Roe Series

Foreword

The Tolkien Society is a charity based in the UK that has the aim of promoting research into, and educating the public in, the life and works of J.R.R. Tolkien. For over 50 years the Society has worked to publish the latest thinking and research on Tolkien's works, and a cornerstone of this is the *Peter Roe* series which regularly showcases the proceedings of our Seminars.

Since this publication was first printed in 1992, technology has developed enough that print-on-demand is now an option, and so our recent *Peter Roe* books – numbers 17, 18 and 19 – have been published by our partners Luna Press Publishing in this way. Now, we are able to republish older *Peter Roe* books that have long since fallen out of print, and make them available in the same format to a new generation of scholars and readers.

This book, *Peter Roe* no 3, *The First and Second Ages*, was first published by the Society in 1992, and constitutes the proceedings of the Tolkien Society Seminar held at the David Baxter Centre in Milton Keynes on 2nd June 1990. Edited by Trevor Reynolds, this edition reproduces the original text apart from a few errors that existed in the original version. As you will see from the contents, the four articles are the talks as delivered at that Seminar to an audience, and perhaps do not read quite as more conventionally scholarly. However, that should not put you off!

The first article – "From Fëanor to Doctor Faustus: A 'Creator' destroys himself" by John Ellison contains an interesting discussion about Fëanor and Faust, and how this leads to self-destruction, including a strong parallel between Sauron and Fëanor in the making of the One Ring and the Silmarils respectively, leading to the ultimate defeat of both. The second article by Denis Bridoux, "Before the Moon, Before the Sun: The Big Time in Tolkien's Mythology" talks about the understanding of time and the world before the arrival of Elves and Men, and in particular, how "literal" we should interpret Tolkien's mythology and whether we should be careful in shining a light too closely on it. The third article, "Purity and Danger in Middle-earth", by Chris Seeman is about the nature of good, evil, power and corruption within Tolkien's world – particularly the First Age – and uses the work of Mary Douglas as a framework for analysing this. And the final article by former Society chairman Alex Lewis, "'Good People': Elves of the First Age" discusses the very different behaviour and temperament of the Elves we see in *The Silmarillion* with those we see in *The Lord of the Rings*, a juxtaposition that many readers have also wrestled with.

What all of these have articles have in common is, as the title of this book says, they are rooted in the First and Second Ages of the legendarium; but there is also a theme here about what constitutes "good" within Tolkien's works. How do we see morality within Tolkien's works and how does that advance our understanding of his creation and his thinking? This is an enduring topic in Tolkien scholarship, which is why I am delighted to be able to present this republication of this book.

Shaun Gunner
Tolkien Society Chair
August 2020

From Fëanor to Doctor Faustus:
A "Creator" destroys himself

By John Ellison

Two years ago we met, as we are doing today, to hold what has come to be the chief annual, "academic" event of the Tolkien Society's calendar. This was, then, the "Workshop", held at Cambridge under the title of "Tolkien and Romanticism" (Morus *et al.*, 1988). Such a theme could of course have provided subject-matter for several "Workshops", and it certainly was not due to any shortcoming in the proceedings themselves, or on anyone's part, that its scope could not be fully explored within the compass of one such event only. It might have seemed strange to some, but it was nevertheless quite understandable, that no one, at the time, touched on or mentioned that most characteristic accompaniment of Romanticism, the legend of Faust. Having devoted myself at the time to quite another aspect of the theme of "Tolkien and Romanticism" (Ellison, 1988), I am now assuming responsibility for what may be called a piece of unfinished business.

Last year we met again at Beverley, and the proceedings were notable above all for the remarkable interpretation by Tom Shippey (1991), in his talk at the "Beverley Workshop", of the significance of "The Homecoming of Beorhtnoth Beorhthelm's Son" (Tolkien 1975) in relation to Tolkien's work and thought.

Its outstanding feature as those who heard Professor Shippey's talk will recall, was its emphasis on the ambivalence of Tolkien's attitude towards "the Northern world", and towards "the Northern heroic spirit", the mainsprings of his creative imagination. He argued that Tolkien in "The Homecoming" is going against his own predilections in siding with Tídwald, the party to the dialogue who takes a cynical and critical view of Beorhtnoth's "heroic" behaviour in voluntarily staking the issue of battle. The implications of this, he suggested, seemed to be that Tolkien had come to regard the "Northern heroic spirit" as something "heathen", in essence; something retaining a destructive element in its make-up which required taming, or in other words, "Christianising" to exorcise it. This feeling on Tolkien's part, he added, might reflect contemporary events in the "real" world at the time "The Homecoming" was written. The degradation of the Northern spirit represented by what had just passed in Nazi Germany was sufficiently plain, but Tolkien might have been even more affected, he thought, by what he saw of the state of the immediate post-war world.

Shippey's talk considerably sharpened my own sense of something peculiarly final and valedictory about Tolkien's own kind of romanticism, and its realisation in his imaginary world. I do not think that the importance of the outbreak, course, and aftermath of the First World War, as the historical context within which Tolkien's mythology was originally conceived and evolved, can be overestimated. Within these years the old pre-1914 certainties of life, as Tolkien and everyone around him would have known them, had collapsed and vanished. He was, as is well known, profoundly and personally affected in the most shattering way, as all the combatants were. The original "Lost Tales" may have been, in the beginning, set down in an "escapist" kind of spirit, that seems more than understandable in the light of the circumstances in which the earliest of them were written. It did not however take very long before Tolkien's "other world" began to "act up at him", in a "non-escapist" ambiguous fashion. A "romantic" he may have been, but he had to face the consequences of romanticism in its decline and passing; and it does not have to be said how disastrous for mankind some of them have turned out to be. The combination of romantic nostalgia for the fading and passing beauties of this world shot through with the apprehension of potential horror underlying them is a recurring element in the arts of the period preceding 1914; very much evident in, say, the symphonies of Elgar or of Mahler, to take a couple of instances.

The particular myth that embrace the entire of Romanticism from its beginning to its final convulsions is known to everyone as the legend of Faust. Embodied at the outset in the two parts of Goethe's poetic drama, it finishes up by denying itself in Thomas Mann's novel *Doctor Faustus*, set against the backdrop of Nazi Germany in its final stages of collapse, a novel that consciously presents itself as an antithesis of, or, "deconstruction" of, Goethe's masterpiece. It was a re-reading on my part of *Doctor Faustus*, that provided the final impulse for this paper. In between the two extremes, the Faust myth, mainly of course Goethe's realisation of it, provided a rich source of artistic inspiration and a quarry for source material, notably in the music, the quintessentially "romantic" art.[1] The infinite potential of the creative human mind both for good and

---

1. Composers who drew on it, from Goethe's own time and subsequently have included Schubert, Mendelssohn, Schumann, Liszt, Wagner, Berlioz, Gounod, Boito, Mahler, Busoni, and Havergal Brian; this list is probably nothing like comprehensive.

evil in the consequences of man's endless search for knowledge, continually simulated and inspired the finest artistic minds.

It occurred to me that it might be worthwhile to look at Tolkien's imagined world against this kind of background. I have to make it clear that it is not my intention to attempt to stage a revival of the once popular, and now rather *passé* pastime of detecting "influences on Tolkien", supposedly derived from various likely and unlikely sources. He would presumably have been conversant, at least to some extent, with the early origins of the legend of Faust, as exemplified in Marlowe's 1604 play, even though he probably had little direct interest as far as that was concerned. How well he knew either part of Goethe's Faust, or both parts, I have not the slightest idea. As far as this paper is concerned, it does not matter at all. On the other hand, the "Faust myth", in one form or another, had become so much a part of every educated person's consciousness by the time Tolkien started out to build his imaginary world, that he could not wholly have escaped its consequences, even had he so wished. Its presence is felt in his work as one of the many background flavourings in "the Soup" – this metaphor of Tolkien's may seem as if it has been a little overworked, but its usefulness is undeniable. The individual manifestation of the "Faust myth", that is of the greatest interest from our present point of view is, as it happens, the very one which post-dates everything in Middle-earth up to the completion of *The Lord of the Rings*, Mann's novel, about which he can have known nothing whatever. I intend to come back to it at the end of this paper, as a means of indicating the peculiar kind of "relevance" Tolkien's imagined world bore and still bears to the concerns of the "real" world in which he lived and worked, concerns which still trouble us today as profoundly as they did him and his contemporaries. I have, though, to start at the point where the peculiar "split" in Tolkien's creative personality, the kind of self-doubt upon which Tom Shippey focused in relation to "Beorhtnoth", first seem to appear. As the mythology is developed and extended over the years, this "split" comes to be defined above all by the way in which the Elves and Orcs are seen more and more as linked opposites, projections of the creative and destructive sides of the human personality. But this concept took shape gradually, as I think, over a long period. It is fully present by the time Frodo's words to Sam, in the Tower of Cirith Ungol, come to be spoken. "The Shadow that bred them can only mock, it cannot make: not real new things of its own. I don't it gave life to the orcs, it only ruined them and twisted them..." (Tolkien, 1966c, 190), whereas it has not fully emerged if looked at in in the light of Treebeard's well-known statement that "Trolls are only counterfeits made by the Enemy in the Great Darkness, as Orcs were of Elves." (Tolkien, 1966b, 189).[2] I suggest that the first important evidence of the "split" is represented by the appearance in "The Tales" of Fëanor. When one looks at the mythology, at the "legendarium" as a whole (if it is indeed a whole), it at once becomes plain that Fëanor occupies a central place in it. He is the key-figure, the hinge on which the whole great Tale, the compendium of the individual Tales, turns.

It of course hardly needs saying that Tolkien's "legendarium" does not contain a Faust-figure as such. No one person enters into a "contract" with Melkor, or with Sauron, or barters his

---

2. The surface inconsistency between these two passages has led to some difficulties in interpretation. Tolkien himself (Tolkien, 1981, 190) insists that in the latter passage, "made" is to be distinguished from "created", but in the former one "make" is clearly synonymous with "create".

soul in exchange for knowledge, power riches, or anything else. (Presumably the Mouth of Sauron has a "contract of service" of some kind, but he can hardly be described as a central figure; the Nine Mortal Men enslaved by the nine Rings may, if you like, represent an unconscious use of a "Faust-motive".) Nevertheless there does seem to be something rather Faust-like about the way Fëanor's career resolves itself into a struggle to transcend the limitations of his own existence: "For man must strive, and striving he must err" (Goethe 1959a, 41) says Goethe's Almighty in the dialogue with Mephistopheles at the beginning of Part I of "Faust"; Fëanor is however an Elf, one of the Elder Children of Ilúvatar who have been confined "within the circles of the world", and perhaps his tragedy is that he was not born a Man instead. The Eldar are summoned by the Valar to dwell in Aman; they are expected to create (or, if the word can be preferred, "sub-create"), in imitation of Eru. In the end most of them prove unable to remain within the bounds that have been set for them. And this had been foreseen. At the time of the summons, Ulmo, in the council of the Valar, had spoken against it, "thinking it were better for the Quendi to remain in Middle-earth" (Tolkien, 1977, 59).

The "restlessness" of the Eldar, of the Noldor especially, is the outward symbol and expression of their creative spirit. Fëanor represents that creativity raised to the highest possible degree. He sits, as it were, on the top of the pile; of the three races of the Eldar who go to Aman, it is the Noldor who are "beloved of Aulë" (Tolkien, 1977, 60). In the search for knowledge, "they soon surpassed their teachers" (Tolkien, 1977, 60), an extremely significant remark. In due time Fëanor surpasses everyone else. His mother Míriel has previously surpassed all her own kindred in her own craft of weaving and needlework, and her strength then passes into Fëanor himself. Rúmil of Tirion is the first of the Noldor to devise letters and musical notation, but Fëanor thereafter surpasses him in the devising of the Fëanorian script. This must indeed represent the truest part played by the Noldor, and by Fëanor himself, in the history of Arda. It has much more significance, really, than the fashioning of jewels, of even of the Silmarils themselves, for writing and letters are the foundation of civilisation, as Tolkien and all the rest of us know and have known it, just as they were the foundation of his creative and professional life. Fëanor's name means "Spirit of Fire", and the imagery of fire pervades the record of his deeds and ending; it is in him, as ever, the classic symbol of creativity; "Oh for a Muse of fire that will ascend the brightest heaven of invention." he is also "*Curufinwë*", and the "curu" element in this name signifying "skill", passes on to one of his sons who inherits the largest measure of it, but not for the better. "Curufin the crafty"; at quite an early stage in the formation of the "legendarium", Tolkien is using his own linguistic mode to point the link between the creative and the destructive in human nature; the English words "craft" and "crafty", of course embody the same inherent ambiguity. I would say that this is the point at which the "split" in Tolkien's attitude to his own handiwork first comes out in the open. Later on the same linguistic ambiguity is to be used to indicate the personality of Saruman, "Man of Skill", coupled with the double meaning of "Orthanc", which in the language of the Mark signifies "The Cunning Mind".

There seems to be a sort of tragic inevitability inherent in the course of Fëanor's existence until his final "dissolution" (if there is no better word for it). He could not have been and could not have done, perhaps, any other than what he was, and did. His career presents the spectacle of a swift ascent to a peak, the fashioning of the Silmarils, which is at the same time a fatally decisive action which sets him on a downward path towards extinction. It is instructive to trace this mythological "rake's progress", in all its successive stages. Significantly, the devising of the Fëanorian script, which betters the work of Fëanor's predecessor Rúmil, and which represents Fëanor's "true" place in the history of Arda, is an achievement of his youth. Subsequently he is first among the Noldor to discover how gems "greater and brighter than those of the Earth", may be made with skill. There is an important distinction to be made between these two feats. The first one is an improvement on art. The second one, more perilous, is an improvement on nature herself.

Fëanor then marries, and Nerdanel his wife, gifted with a higher measure of patience, tries to restrain his over-enthusiastic spirit, in the end unsuccessfully. Her more moderate nature passes, to some extent, to some, but not all, of her sons. Fëanor himself extends the range of his creative enterprise, and his father-in-law Mahtan instructs him in the making of things in metal and stone. When his father Finwë remarries, he develops antipathy towards his stepmother, and then to his new half-brothers, and withdraws into his own concerns.

At this stage Melkor is pardoned by the Valar after three Ages of Arda, and is allowed to dwell in Aman. Fëanor develops a special hatred of him, and first names him "Morgoth" ("Dark Enemy"). Amateur psychology might at this point indicate that what he is actually doing is to embark on the dangerous course of denying the "dark" side of his own nature, pushing back his "destructive" self into unconscious. Be that as it may, his own nature seems destined to lead him into some kind of "special relationship" with Melkor, even if the contractual element, binding Faust to Mephistopheles, is absent, or at least, seems, on the surface, to be absent. The making of the Silmarils follows directly upon the unchaining of Melkor. Tolkien at this point drops a hint of the tragedy inevitably lying ahead; "it may be", he says, "that some shadow of foreknowledge came to him of the doom that drew near." (Tolkien, 1977, 67). The lust and envy of Melkor are roused, and he embarks on the seduction of the Noldor, who begin to "murmur against the Valar". Fëanor himself begins to look outside Aman; it now seems that his interests and inclinations have undergone a major change of direction. "Fiercest burned the new flame of desire for freedom and wider realms in the eager heart of Fëanor" (Tolkien, 1977, 68). The "flame" may be a new one, but it does not appear to be a flame of creativity. He guards the Silmarils in his own hoard and treats them as his own property; "he seldom remembered now that the light within them was not his own" (Tolkien, 1977, 69).

The next following sequence of events makes the deterioration in his moral stance quite plain. It starts with him turning his craft and skills to the making of a secret forge, and to using it to produce weapons of war; he makes swords and helmets for himself and his sons. Mahtan, his father-in-law, now regrets having taught him the skill in metalworking that he himself originally learned from Aulë. In this rebellious mood he begins to speak openly against the Valar, and an open breach follows with his half-brother Fingolfin; the result of this is that he is summoned to appear before the Valar, and receives a sentence of banishment. This does not appear to have any effect on him. He retires to Formenos and makes a fortress and a hoard of weapons and treasure there, locking the

Silmarils in a chamber of iron. At this point Melkor appears there and confronts him; with the apparent intention of playing Mephistopheles to Fëanor's Faust, he tries to enlist him on his own side. However, as it happens, he overplays his hand. In the midst of his efforts to inflame Fëanor's rage and his suspicions of the Valar, he allows his own lust for the Silmarils to show itself. He leaves Formenos with the Northern heroic equivalent of a flea in his ear.

We now arrive at the central sequence of events which represents the Darkening of Valinor. Fëanor is summoned to Valmar from Formenos, and while he is there the assault of Melkor and Ungoliant upon the Two Trees takes place. Fëanor withholds it. To break them, he says, in effect would mean breaking him as well; "never again shall I make their like". Melkor has meanwhile reached Formenos, slain Finwë, Fëanor's father, and taken the Silmarils. This would have happened in any case, says the Tale, whether Fëanor had refused Yavanna or not. "Yet had he said yea to Yavanna at first, before the tidings came from Formenos, it may be that his after deeds would have been other than they were" (Tolkien, 1977, 79). There has been, therefore, a moment of decisive choice; after it, Fëanor's path is set irreversibly downward towards destruction. I will return to the actual words he speaks later on, and quote them then, as they relate closely to the main theme of this paper.

The pace of events now begins to accelerate. Fëanor appears in Túna and inflames the Noldor to revolt. "Fierce and fell were his words, and filled with anger and pride, and hearing them the Noldor were stirred to madness." (Tolkien, 1977, 82). I am not sure exactly when Tolkien wrote these words, but their "applicability" to the 1930s is rather striking. This exercise of the power of mob-oratory is followed by the theatrical, not to say operatic scene of the oath-taking of Fëanor and his sons; they swear to pursue the Silmarils to the ends of the earth. Dissension breaks out, and Fëanor is opposed by Fingolfin and Turgon, and also with more moderation by Finarfin, but his side prevails in the end, and the Noldor prepare to depart and set out for Middle-earth. The herald of Manwë appears, bent on restraining their departure, but his words of warning are ignored, and Fëanor's response to him contains significant words which will turn out to have given to the familiar imagery a new and sinister emphasis. "It may be", says Fëanor, "that Eru has set in me a fire greater than thou knowest." (Tolkien, 1977, 85). What this new fire may be will soon become clear.

The following sequence of events alienates Fëanor permanently from all the rest of the Eldar except those of his own house. These comprise: the parley with the Teleri at Alqualondë, the subsequent battle with them and the Kinslaying; the escape of the Noldor in the ships of the Teleri; the judgement passed on them, and signalled to them on their subsequent road, recorded as "The Prophecy of the North"; and finally the crossing of the Helcaraxë and subsequently, the burning of the ships at Fëanor's orders. Their return across the straits is rendered impossible, and the subsequent passage across the straits of the section of the host led by Fingolfin has to be undertaken and achieved without them. By this time Fëanor appears to accept the inevitability of his own "doom", and even to welcome it; the "Northern heroic spirit" in him has now reached its highest level of intensity. With the burning of the ships the symbolism of "The Spirit of Fire" has reached a wholly destructive stage; at this point the words "he laughed as one fey", are applied to him; the epithet will recur at the time of

11

his death. This word *fey*, like other characteristics of Tolkien's "archaic" or "high" style, is used to convey a kind of coded meaning for which "mad" is a wholly inadequate equivalent.[3]

Fëanor's end is not long in coming once the Noldor have arrived in Middle-earth. It takes place not in the actual battle, the Dagor-nuin-Giliath, that quickly follows, but in its aftermath. The battle itself is a victory, and the remaining Orcs flee from the field in retreat. Fëanor alone presses on in their wake, senselessly and unnecessarily. It is his last and most typical piece of "Beorhtnothery", if one may be allowed to coin the word. "He was fey", says Tolkien, "consumed by the flame of his own wrath." He is finally smitten to the ground and fatally wounded. Borne back by his sons towards Mithrim he dies looking out from afar at the peaks of Thangorodrim, and "so fiery was his spirit that as it sped his body fell to ash, and was borne away like smoke." (Tolkien, 1977, 107). The new fire of which he boasted to the herald of Manwë as the host prepared to depart from Túna has turned on him and consumed him at last.

It is not evident from Fëanor's life-history that the making of the Silmarils constitutes both the peak of it, and its single catastrophic error? He ensnared the light of the Two Trees, a universal light in which no "property" existed. The deterioration in his character started to show itself as soon as he had made the Silmarils, in the possessiveness that overtook him from that time on. The underlying cause of it was his realising that he had made something which he himself could not surpass. He could not strive after perfection any longer; he had achieved

---

3. For those who know Wagner's *Die Meistersinger*, the untranslatable word "Wahn" (illusion), which implies a combination of insanity, frenzy, and delusion, both private and public, perhaps comes quite close to it.

it, and all that "creation" could represent for him after that, was mere pattern-making. The essence of creativity is not perfection, but the tireless search for it; Faust was required to strive ceaselessly and never to pause to contemplate "the passing moment". Fëanor's words at the time of his refusal to Yavanna's plea for the aid of the Silmarils show that he has betrayed himself into falling in love with the work of his own hand: "For the less even as for the greater there is some deed that he may accomplish but once only, and in that deed his heart shall rest." (Tolkien, 1977, 78). This is the equivalent of the fatal words that in Faust's contract with Mephistopheles were to doom him.

"Then to the moment I can say
Linger you now, you are so fair."
(Goethe, 1959b, 270)

("Verweile doch, du bist so schön".) (I have deliberately misquoted the words which Faust actually does speak just before his death in Part II of "Faust". Goethe, at the last minute, replaced "can say" with "could say", so that Faust escapes damnation by a hairsbreadth; and is shown as redeemed in the final scene of "Faust".)

From Tolkien's own point of view, I believe that Fëanor's making of the Silmarils represented a dangerous and impermissible act, one that exceeded the bounds intended for the Elder Children of Ilúvatar. I do not of course suggest that there is any autobiographical element about his concept of Fëanor's character; that would be absurd. I think, on the other hand, that he sensed that there could be a certain applicability to his own situation about it, and that this affected his subsequent attitude towards his own creative work. The word "fey", as it appears in relation to Fëanor, does, as it happens, have an exact counterpart in the German original equivalent of Tolkien's own name, *tollkühn*. I do not mean that he thought that either epithet in either language was in any way applicable to himself, but he can hardly have been unaware of the linguistic implications. These will, incidentally, present us towards the end of this paper with an exceedingly picturesque coincidence. The outward sign of all this is the curious appearance of inhibition which seems to characterise Tolkien's attitude to his imaginative writing. At a superficial level he was probably worried about what his professional colleagues might say if they knew about it. They would accuse him of "wasting his time on this sort of stuff", while he ought to have been getting on with his scholastic work. At a deeper level, there may have been something about the whole idea of "creativity" that conflicted with his deeply ingrained religious sense. He needed to rationalise and justify his own position, to legitimise his invention, to enable him to carry on writing. He did so by evolving the idea of "sub-creation", set down in the Andrew Lang lecture, later essay, "On Fairy-Stories" (Tolkien, 1964). The artist is seen as a sort of feudal tenant-in-chief of a medieval king, making his own little world in imitation of the one into which he himself is made. The subordinate, or "sub-creative", role allotted to the individual as artist, contrasts very strongly with the assumption of overriding status as belonging to the art-form itself, the writing of fantasy. Tolkien might have felt inhibited about acknowledging his own status as an artist; but that does not imply that he thought that what he was doing was not supremely important.

This sense of "perfection", or completeness, as something to be shunned as much as possible, seems manifest in Tolkien's notorious disinclination (I do not believe it was inability) to finish anything. From "The Book of Lost Tales" on, not a single major project is carried all the way to completion; some of course come within a reasonable distance of it. He finished *The Hobbit*, but he had to be prodded into doing that, and of course he never regarded that work in the same light as his long-term preoccupation with his older mythology – it wasn't at the heart of his imaginative thinking as *The Silmarillion* was. The single major exception to the rule turns out to be no exception at all. Tolkien did not think of *The Lord of the Rings* as something independently complete in itself, but rather as the last leaf of a triptych of which large sections of the other two leaves remained unfulfilled. He expended some twenty-odd closely packed pages in outlining the whole panorama to Milton Waldman (Tolkien, 1981, 143-161), and also, for a time, drove George Allen and Unwin Ltd. nearly frantic by insisting that *The Silmarillion* was as large as *The Lord of the Rings*, of equal importance, and that it consequently should be published in tandem with it. Niggle's Tree, in other words, can never be completed in this "fallen" world; it would encourage presumptuousness to believe otherwise.

Another piece of Tolkien's writing that I suspect also bears some relation to this aspect of his thought, is "The Lay of Aotrou and Itroun" (Tolkien, 1945). I am not trying to offer anything like a cut-and-dried interpretation of this piece, but it has always struck me as a rather strange choice of subject from Tolkien's point of view, unless one postulates a kind of applicability about the tale to an artist's creativity. The physical act of procreation is, after all, a common enough metaphor for it; many painters (Turner for instance), writers or composers have thought of or referred to their pictures or their books or their scores as their "children". The Lord Aotrou, in his desire for posterity, breaks the bounds of what is "allowable" or legitimate, laid down by his religion, as Fëanor tried to exceed the bounds prescribed for the Eldar in Aman. The remarkable feature of the tale, from the present point of view, however, is that the motive of a contract with the Devil, or the Devil's representative, is genuinely present. His punishment, when the bargain proves impossible to fulfil, occurs, as far as we can tell, in this world, not in the next; but perhaps he is the closest approach to a Faust figure in Tolkien's writing, even if only in miniature. We will also be encountering the Corrigan, the witch as the Devil's representative, shortly again, playing the same role in a twentieth century context.

Further reasons for giving "The Tale of Fëanor" (I call it that for convenience's sake), a central place in the structure of Tolkien's thought lies in the way its essence seems to recur in two principal Tales of the Second and Third Ages: the rise and fall of Númenor, and the History of the One Ring. I will briefly indicate some ways in which they seem to correspond. The Dúnedain, once they are settled in Númenor, develop a rich and complex civilisation. While they are passing through the early stages of the formation of their culture, they derive much from the Eldar in Eressëa, and in the west of Middle-earth. They learn their language and take from them their nomenclature. Then they begin to surpass their teachers, as the Eldar had previously done, emerging from the tutelage of the Valar. The particular occupation which symbolises their creative spirit and creative powers is shipbuilding and seacraft. As mariners and "men of peace", they first bring their civilisation to the shores of Middle-earth. The port and harbour of Vinyalondë and other outposts are set up through which trading and other relations with the indigenous and other peoples of the mainland develop and are fostered. This in retrospect seems like a kind of Renaissance period in Middle-earth in the Second Age; an outburst of creative energy comparable to the expansion of Europe at the close of the Middle Ages. The final years of Númenor's history might likewise be thought of in terms of that of the first half of the twentieth century, to the rise of the tyrannies, fascism, Stalinism, and the destruction of the old "bourgeois, liberal and humanist" Europe in two world wars. There is an obvious "applicability" which presumably Tolkien had no conscious thought of expressing. Men in Middle-earth who at first had been civilised by the Númenóreans, when the latter ultimately come as warriors and overlords, are instead terrorized.

The Tale of Aldarion and Erendis, within the compass of one particular story and one set of events, is a kind of parable of Númenórean history, a commentary on its progress from its beginnings to the final downfall. The destructive element is Aldarion's insistence on pressing on with his shipbuilding schemes and his voyages in defiance both of his public and personal obligations. It is a classic instance of the kind of presumptuousness[4] that has been the undoing of Fëanor, and represents "creativity" out of control, turning on its possessor, with consequences not merely personal but also fatal for society as a whole. Erendis's abandonment by Aldarion and the resulting strangeness of her relationship with her daughter,

4. Or "ofermod" in the Old English equivalent, translated by Tolkien as "overmastering pride". It is no less applicable to Fëanor himself.

have consequences for the Númenórean succession which ultimately issue forth in the last catastrophe. In the end the last Númenórean king challenges the might of Sauron and another "special relationship" ensues. The largest armada ever seen is built and launched; the Ban of the Valar is broken, and the world is changed. This is not the climax of an "action replay" of the Tale of Fëanor, but there is a notable similarity of outline and underlying meaning.

The History of the One Ring might on the other hand be seen as standing in an inverted relationship with the Tale of Fëanor; turning it upside-down with, at its centre, the One Ring as a "debased" counterpart of the Silmarils. The latter represented an ideal of beauty and perfection, and as such only presented a threat to those who held them with intent to possess them; then their effects were instantaneously felt, those who held them being tormented with physical pain. (The One Ring operates in a precisely contrary way, producing an apparent beneficial physical effect to start with, and fostering possessiveness, not repelling it.)

Maedhros and Maglor, the two of Fëanor's sons who have inherited the largest measure of his "positive" creative qualities, become in the end the most tragic of them. They make their way into the camp of Eönwë, after the Last Battle with Morgoth in which the two remaining Silmarils have been recovered, and make off with them. The hollowness of the claim of Fëanor and his house to ownership is at once apparent to them, and in their torment they are forced to cast them away. The death of Maedhros, casting a Silmaril and himself into a crack of fire in the earth, which clearly anticipates Gollum's end in Orodruin, provides a highly significant link between the two Tales. Maglor's torment is that of the artist who realises

18

the unattainability of an ideal; he cats a Silmaril into the sea and "wanders ever singing in pain and regret beside the waves" (Tolkien, 1977, 254), one of the most haunting images in Tolkien's works.

If the Silmarils enshrine ideal beauty, the One Ring enshrines its opposite: power. As a complementary counterpart of the Silmarils it too is beautiful to look on, at least outwardly: "of all the works of Sauron the only fair". It represents the debasement of creativity; the values of true art turned upside-down; the cacophony introduced by Melkor into the Music of the Ainur. Its making links it firmly with the history of Fëanor and the Fëanorians, through Celebrimbor, the chief of the Elvensmith of Eregion, and the son of Curufin "the crafty" who "desired in his heart to rival the skill and fame of Fëanor" (Tolkien, 1980b, 236). The Elvensmiths traffic with Sauron in the Second Age, and obtain his instruction in the making of rings, at first the lesser ones, and in the end the Three Rings forged by Celebrimbor himself, whose existence leads to the forging of the One Ring by Sauron "to rule them all". There is perhaps even a sense in which the War of the Ring may be thought of as a "War of the Silmarils" in reverse, viewed from the other side, the Enemy's side. Sauron has to wage it in order to regain, in his turn, the work of his own hand which has been taken from him, and his war, like that of the Elves in Beleriand, becomes a "long defeat".

Tolkien's world, as principally represented by Fëanor's part in it, and as seen against a late romantic background, may seem to display some congruences with the legend of Faust, or echoes of it, but not to provide an exact or comprehensive equivalent. Fëanor, up to now, may be thought to qualify as a "Faust figure" of a sort, but the relationship is not quite a direct one, but lies at a tangent. I now come, though, to review the particular version of the legend of Faust that started me off on this enquiry. This is Thomas Mann's novel *Doctor Faustus*, and to those who know it the comparison may initially seem a very strange one indeed. Tolkien's world existed and exists entirely in his imagination, and in ours; its relation to, or connections with, his and our contemporary world, and with history as it was being made at the time of its own making, arise (assuming that they arise at all) purely by implication. Thomas Mann in *Doctor Faustus* (written at nearly the same time as *The Lord of the Rings*), is concerned, on the other hand, with the crisis in the culture and identity of his own country at a catastrophic period in its history; he employs a multiplicity of allusive devices to make it appear even more "historical" than it is. Nevertheless, it represents the point at which Tolkien's "mythology" and the "Faust myth" actually intersect. I cannot think of a better way of putting it than by saying that the hero, or rather "anti-hero", of *Doctor Faustus*, the imaginary composer Adrian Leverkühn, is a Fëanor of our times, a Fëanor playing out his role as a symbol and key-figure of the crisis of the first half of the twentieth century, the aftermath and end-product of Romanticism.

At this point I have to provide an outline of the content of *Doctor Faustus*, in order to make the above comparison, and the reasons underlying it, seem at all understandable. It will have to be an exceedingly rough outline. *Doctor Faustus* is a long and complex work, and full of allusions and references at every turn to Mann's own world: the Germany which he left in 1933, just after Hitler's assumption of power. However, the complex detail does not really affect the issue for the present purpose.

The story is that of the life of a composer, Adrian Leverkühn, told by his closest friend. It is now that the picturesque coincidence arises, which I mentioned previously. Mann chose the name of his hero consciously, to indicate his personality. "*Leverkühn*" ("living audaciously") is a partial congruence with "*tollkühn*", it would be appropriate as characterising Fëanor, at least in the early part of his career. (Mann's actual allusion is to Nietzsche and Zarathustra, although that does not concern us here.) Serenus Zeitblom, the narrator, is depicted as telling his friend's life-story at the time when his own world is collapsing in ruins around him; he "writes" as from within Nazi Germany during the closing stages of the Second World War. (This is an interesting parallel to Tolkien's setting out to build his mythology while surrounded by the evidences of the collapse of the old pre-1914 world, including his own part of it.) Zeitblom is a teacher by profession, and represents the archetypal "Good German", brought up within the old bourgeois world of German culture: "the land of poets and thinkers", of Goethe and Schiller, of Bach and Beethoven. (In Númenórean terms, he is one of "the Faithful".) The early part of the book recounts Leverkühn's upbringing and musical training; the stages through which he develops to attain technical mastery of the essentials of his art. His teacher, the organist Wendell Kretzschmar, is a kind of benevolent father-figure to him; one whose tutelage he is destined to outgrow, as the Noldor "surpassed their teachers". He initially cannot see a future for himself in music, and turns to studying theology for some intervening years. Eventually he resumes his studies in music and composition, but he still sees no future for himself as a creative artist, constrained as he is within the discipline under which he has been brought up. (His budding genius has been apparent from the beginning.) That discipline of course is the mainstream of German music through Bach and Beethoven and the "early romantics" up to Wagner and the end of the nineteenth century, and for Leverkühn the challenge is to "break out of it", in order that his composing shall be more than mere pattern-making.

The episode which represents his "breaking out" also symbolises his contract with the Devil. It is, on the surface, only the fact of his having consorted with a prostitute (the "Corrigan" of Aotrou and Itroun in another shape), or his being assumed to have done so; the incident is not directly narrated. There is another factual allusion here – to Nietzsche, who died insane, supposedly as a result of syphilis contracted when still a student. Leverkühn is to become insane in the last years of his life, and the fate is a traditional one for composers of the romantic era. There is a parallel symbolic allusion to the "intellectuals" in Germany who "gave themselves" to authoritarianism and Nazism in the 1920s and 1930s. The effect of Leverkühn's encounter with "the Corrigan", is to release his individual voice as a musician. His music develops along unprecedented lines, and a succession of works show him evolving a new method of composition – a new musical system which will replace the old. A feature of his new music is that the letters of the prostitute's name HETAERA[5] ESMERALDA, translated into notes, make up a musical code which recurs repeatedly in his works. The "new musical system", which Leverkühn invents so as to replace the old, is actually a deliberate "calque",[6]

5. A title – it refers to the "professional prostitute" class in Athens of the fifth century BC.

6. See T A Shippey (1982, 77-8), (where the Shire, for instance, is described as "calqued" on England) for an explanation of the term. In Thomas Mann's case the "calque" infuriated many of Schönberg's followers; the description

or imitation of musical history as it happened in reality. The "real-life" model is the exhaustion of the old tonal system (the major and minor keys and their relations with each other), and the "serial", or "twelve-tone", system pioneered by Arnold Schönberg with the intention of replacing it.

There is, however, a horrific price to be paid for Leverkühn's new-found freedom. His "new musical system" is the outcome of "devilish" inspiration, and in a section in the middle of the book the Devil himself appears to Leverkühn to explain the nature of the bond that now exists between them. This passage has, of course, to be understood as symbolic, not real; it is not part of Zeitblom's narrative but is told as though it has been reconstructed afterwards, from what Leverkühn himself, displaying early signs of insanity, has written down about it. Its message is the inversion of all pre-existing musical values. Sublimity, solemnity and order, are henceforth to be represented by discord and dissonance; harmony and consonance will stand only for chaos, confusion, disorder; in a word, Hell. The formal rules of composition in the "New Order" in music (one could call it a "Music of the Ainur", newly devised by Melkor), are nevertheless to be absolute, "totalitarian" in their strictness and rigidity. All of this represents, at one level, a political allegory, for the "New Order" in music is to be equated with the barbarism of the "New Order" in Europe; the rule of the Thousand-Year Reich.

Leverkühn's career as a composer reaches his climax with his

---

of Leverkühn's music in the novel do not really suggest anything very much like orthodox "twelve-tone" music, as it became known. Mann also introduced the names of "real" musicians (the conductors Otto Klemperer and Bruno Walter and the tenor Karl Erb) as performers of Leverkühn's imaginary works.

final masterpiece, the "symphonic cantata", "The Lamentation of Doctor Faustus". Mann's account of this imaginary work, perhaps the most remarkable piece of descriptive writing about music ever produced by a non-musician, draws the sharpest possible contrast between the "totalitarian" strictness of the new system within which it is composed – "there was no longer any free note", he says – and the intense subjectivity of its emotional expression. But the only emotions it expresses are those of utter agony and despair; like Maglor, Leverkühn's Faust is doomed "ever to wander singing in pain and regret beside the waves". As Mann himself in *Doctor Faustus* has "unwritten" the Faust of Goethe, so does Leverkühn in his final masterpiece symbolically "unwrite" Beethoven's Ninth Symphony, with its concluding "Ode to Joy", the supreme affirmative symbol of the dawn of the romantic age in music. So appalled is Zeitblom by the unrelieved despair of Leverkühn's masterpiece, that he tries to seek consolation in the void beyond it.

"Expressiveness – expression as lament – is the issue of the whole construction; then may we not parallel it with another, a religious one, and say too (though only in the lowest whisper) that out of the sheerly irremediable hope might germinate? It would be but a hope beyond hopelessness, the transcendence of despair – not betrayal to her, but the miracle that passes belief." (Mann, 1949).

What a thoroughly Tolkienian attitude that it! The very spirit that sustains Frodo and Samwise on their journey into Mordor! It is also the only thing that sustains Zeitblom himself, at the very end of *Doctor Faustus*, as he contemplates the shattered ruin that is all that is left of Germany. "When, out of uttermost hopelessness – a miracle beyond the power of belief – will the light of hope dawn? A lonely man folds his hands and speaks, 'God be merciful to thy poor soul, my friend, my Fatherland!'" (Mann, 1949).

The completion of the work signals Leverkühn physical collapse and the loss of his reason. At a musical gathering at which he is due to play extracts from the work and comment on it, he talks confusedly and nonsensically, confesses the "devilish" origin of his inspiration, and breaks down. He becomes insane and dies in 1940, a few years afterwards.

I hope that some correspondences between Fëanor's "mythological rake's progress", and Adrian Leverkühn's fictional-historical one, emerge reasonably clearly from the foregoing. The history of both is that of genius corrupted finally into insanity; the creative drive turns on its possessor and destroys him, and with him a good part of the fabric of society. Thomas Mann, well before 1933, could witness the spectacle, at close quarters, of civilisation about to slide into barbarism. Tolkien, likewise, had plenty of opportunities for observing and commenting on the same spectacle, or a similar one, and he did so in many and varied ways. For him the sight of green country ruined and despoiled by industrial or commercial development was simply one single manifestation of it; "just another of the works of Mordor". It is noteworthy that Tolkien's letters display no particular satisfaction or any feeling of exultation about the end of the Second World War; rather than that they convey the sense that the underlying situation of mankind has not changed.[7] Above all there is his appalled response to the

---

7. See page 1 for TA Shippey's view of the significance of "The Homecoming of Beorhtnoth Beorhthelm's Son", in this connection.

news of the making of the atomic bomb, and its use on Japan, "Well we're in God's hands. But He does not look kindly on Babel-builders." (Tolkien, 1981, 116.) Here, if you like, is the new "fire set in me, greater than thou knowest", of which Fëanor boasts in his response to the herald of Manwë as the Noldor prepare to leave Aman. It seems quite remarkable in the face of this that there are still people who are prepared to believe that Tolkien's world holds nothing beyond a straightforward conflict between the uncorrupted good and the irredeemably evil. Quite otherwise, he constantly returns to one particular theme; that the creative and destructive forces in man's nature are indivisibly linked; this is the essence of the "fallen world", in which we live. It is not a particularly comforting message, but it is an eminently contemporary one.

Before the Moon Before the Sun:
The Big Time in Tolkien's Mythology

By Denis Bridoux

Although I am perfectly aware that the subject of this Seminar is "The First and Second Ages", I also take it to imply "And What Went On Before" and this is basically the setting for my talk today. I personally do not view this session so much as a talk where a 'learned scholar' would impart his knowledge in a doctrinal tone to a dedicated assembly, as a guided discussion, to which each and every one of you is welcome to contribute, in order to increase and deepen our knowledge in a mutually beneficent manner.

I will thus introduce this session and, in so doing, will raise some questions upon which, I am sure, many of you have pondered upon already and for which I have found no ready answer.

Before I go too far, I wish to emphasise that I am no archaeologist and that my knowledge of the *Big Time* (also known sometimes as Dreamtime) derives solely from my study of Mythology.

The term *Big Time* is usually used by historians and mythologists to refer to a period in the past of a given society, or people, which is shrouded in mystery, or which, although it may have a ready-made history, this history does not seem to tie in with the local archaeology and/or the various annals and chronicles (themselves of somewhat dubious nature sometimes) of the neighbouring people which may have had dealings with them. Why should this be?

For one thing, people always tend to re-write their past histories, improving over the good bits and glossing over the bad ones. Revisionism is not an invention of the Third Reich or George Orwell but has been in existence for as long as histories have been written or told. Why should this be so? The truth is that the further one goes into the past, the more blank does the canvas of history become: this inevitably tends to tempt any 'artist' into filling it up, either, maybe, with snippets of truth linked together with a morass of invention or with elements of religion or mythology which then becomes historicised. On the other hand a reverse process, called euhemerisation, from the Greek philosopher Euhemerus, may take place, whereby historical figures are turned into gods, whether voluntarily, as happened to Egyptian Pharaohs and Roman Emperors, or naturally, over time, when people look back at historical figures and grant the god-like status because of their greater than life activities, as happened to Alexander. Thus Snorri, at the very beginning of The Prose Edda, presented the Norse gods as mighty heroes and wizards of old so befuddled their audience that they became worshipped as gods. A similar occurrence took place with Sauron in the Second Age and probably with the Blue Wizards in the Third Age, with the difference that, in their case, they really were gods within the context of the legendarium, albeit lesser ones, to start with, if one uses the earlier terminology of *Valar* meaning gods.

The words of Kevin Crossley-Holland, in his introduction to his prose retelling of *The Norse Myths* (1980, xxxix-xl), are particularly applicable to Tolkien, for he says:

> "Post-Darwinian societies cannot subscribe to myth as being literally true. It is no longer possible to accept that earth and life on earth broke out of an egg or were shaped by some supernatural potter or, as Norsemen believed, were made from the bodies of a frost-giant and a cow. Perhaps the only real successor to the myth-maker is that poet, philosopher or scientist who is no prisoner of his own methodology but is intent upon discovering origin and function and relationship, a man concerned moreover not only with explicable matter but with spirit. Only he can ever be in a position to recreate the meaning of life for us in the simple yet exalted way that the myth-tellers once did."

Thus Tolkien, who from very early on in his life, had wanted to write a Mythology for England was very familiar with the organic way in which mythology and History are inextricably intertwined, and put his knowledge to good practice from *The Book of Lost Tales* onwards.

Most people, nowadays, apart from religious fundamentalists, would view, for example, the early books of the Bible as either allegorical or symbolic, but most people in pre-Darwinian times thought otherwise: they took every word of it literally. However, to do so tied them in knots from which they could only extricate themselves by invoking "Divine Mystery". In many ways Tolkien presented the tales predating the Arising of the Sun and Moon and, to a lesser extent, those predating the Bending of the World, in a similar manner as is done in those early texts. Is it any wonder that, late in his life, he would attempt to rewrite his Mythology and "make the world always round", thus doing away with all the inconsistencies a flat Earth would entail, for stretching belief too far? The earlier events of the *Legendarium*, those preceding the rise of the Sun and Moon, would gradually be pared down over the decades, as in the case of the lavish description of the making of the vessels of the Sun and Moon themselves in *The Book of Lost Tales* which was changed into the poetic brevity of the same event in *The Silmarillion*, and which leaves much space for the reader's own imagination to flesh it out.

Tolkien's preoccupation was to devise a mythology in which gods really trod the earth, where Elves *really* existed and intermarried with Men, where word and meaning were not separate but one, where metaphors such as "lost as babes in the wood", "burning one's ships" and "teaching your grandmother to suck eggses" were actually true, i.e. where they no longer were simple abstract metaphors but direct depictions of actual events. He thus invited his reader to take every word of his texts literally, as 'gospel truth', as self-consistent, within the context of his *Legendarium*. When presented with Tolkien's universe we are invited to take it as face value, to be, as it were, Tolkienian fundamentalists.

There is much in Tolkien's Legendarium that *is* self-consistent – indeed why should it be otherwise when you think it took him a lifetime to write and rewrite it? – this especially from the time of the Sun and Moon and the Awakening of the Second Children onwards, but, as we recede further and further towards the past, the preceding eras may become increasingly difficult to apprehend at face value, to take literally, without tying ourselves in knots or feeling vaguely dissatisfied. Think for example of the seven Valian years – seventy Sun years – it took for the Noldor to leave Aman and reach Middle-earth, most of them crossing the Helcaraxë on foot! How did they manage to bring enough food with them? Even lembas would not be sufficient for them to survive so long!

Although Time and its reckoning began as such with the first light emerging from Telperion, we may say that time as we know it today began with the first rising of the Sun in the West. All the events preceding are, to all intents and purposes, part of a "Big Time". Indeed, as it appears, the very years were longer, a yen taking 144 of our years – notice here the discrepancy between a Valian year and a yen, which must proceed from different writing stages of "The History of Middle-earth". To the Men who learnt and wrote down the annals of what had gone on before, there must have appeared to be many inconsistencies, which could only be rectified with the additional help of information which, either the Elves themselves did not hold, or which they did not provide either because they thought it irrelevant or simply didn't think of telling them, and because the Men didn't dare asking for further details. As it is, the problems are ours to solve: our task it is to iron out any wrinkle we may see in the cloth, or is it?

For, on the one hand, as Tolkien wrote in a letter somewhere, "the more you write about Elves, the more you turn them into ordinary people", and the same could be said of the Valar of *The Book of Lost Tales*, and yet, on the other, we thirst evermore for further information and endeavour to fill those blank spaces ourselves, to embroider upon the warp and weft of the tapestry with our own thread, and, in so doing, often try to bring together mutually incompatible views.

How, for example, is one to reconcile the concept that in Aman nothing dies but remains ever young and green as in a perpetual Springtime, with the idea of Celegorm and Aredhel, among others, hunting in the company of Oromë in the

Southern parts of Valinor? For one thing, what do they hunt? What are their quarries? Huan, the hound given to Celegorm by Oromë, is a wolf-hound: are there any wolves in Valinor? If so, I would expect them to lie with the lamb, and so not to require hunting. In those days nobody knew the Noldor would return to Middle-earth, so what is a wolf-hound, obviously made for Middle-earth, doing in Valinor? One possible solution might be to imagine that there would be creatures in Valinor solely designed to be hunted – genetic engineering indeed – and to draw enjoyment from it, but that, I think, would be a cop-out in addition to a distasteful concept, at least for myself. Moreover, the problem of pain intervenes: I know that some fishers fish only for fun and release their takings eventually but the situation remains that, in so doing, the fish has been hooked and hurt, and subjected to stress and pain before being released. I personally find the concept of hunting solely for sport repellent, although I cannot disapprove of the concept of hunting for food and clothing purposes. The tale refers to hunts, not mock-hunts anyway. A mock quarry pretending to run away from people pretending to hunt it, that doesn't sound like much fun and, I think, would soon pale! Moreover, people would rapidly grow discontented and rather go for the real thing.

The situation at the time Tolkien wrote *The Book of Lost Tales* was probably totally different, though, and our outlook on hunting is now coloured in the light of animal rights, and we cannot be sure of what Tolkien would have thought of today's animal rights campaigners: I would like to think he might not have remained insensitive to their arguments, without going as far as condoning their action.

It is well known that the theme of the hunt is an ancient one relating to Elves, one which Tolkien made use of from *The*

Book of Lost Tales onwards. One thus recalls the faery host of Gilfanon, lord of Tavrobel, hunting, (tellingly) on Cannock Chase in *The Book of Lost Tales II*. Oromë is, of course, the archetypal hunter: even before the coming of the Elves he used to return to Middle-earth to hunt the fell creatures of Melkor; it is as a hunter that the Elves first see him, and it may be that the resplendent sight of Oromë, riding on golden-shod Nahar, would fire many Elves' imagination. Concurrently, it could be that, in a similar way as he taught the Noldor to fashion weapons, Melkor would also suggest possible uses for them, such as hunting, and that he would remind Celegorm (among others) of Oromë's mighty deeds, and tempt him into doing likewise in Valinor. But the query remains: what did they hunt and why? This, contrary to appearances, is no light matter, for it raises many philosophical problems which are all centred around the very nature of the Blessed Realm.

Another related question, is that of the Elves' diet and vestment, particularly when they still lived in Middle-earth, for hunting was primarily for achieving these two purposes. All the information we seem to have in the Legendarium, from *The Lays of Beleriand* onwards, points towards strict vegetarianism and hunting for meat would thus be pointless. It is said of Beleg, in the first version of the "The Lay of the Children of Húrin", "there baked flesh and bread from his wallet they had to their hearts joy" (Tolkien, 1981, 228) and that he also drew "a flask of leather full filled with wine" (Tolkien, 1981, 224) and of the table of Thingol "that goodly meats there burdened the boards" (Tolkien, 1981, 426), but in the second version of the poem only "wheaten bread to hearts' delight he [Beleg] haled from his wallet", though he still "had a flask of leather full filled with wine"; thus they would then already be vegetarians at this early stage. But *what* would they eat and wear in their early days in Middle-earth before the rising of the Sun? Tolkien seems quite clear about these early days: Chapter One of *The Silmarillion* proper refers to

"the seeds that Yavanna had sown began swiftly to sprout and to burgeon, and there arose a multitude of growing things great and small, mosses and grasses and great ferns, and trees whose tops were crowned with cloud as they were living mountains, but whose feet were wrapped in a green twilight. And beasts came forth, and dwelt in the grassy plains, or in the rivers and the lakes, or walked in the shadows of the woods. As yet no flower had bloomed nor any bird had sung, for these things waited still in the bosom of Yavanna."

and

"green things fell sick and rotted, and rivers were choked with weeds and slime, and fens were made, rank and poisonous, the breeding place of flies; and forests grew dark and perilous, the haunts of fear; and beast became monsters of horns and ivory and dyed the earth with blood."

This, to all intents and purposes, seems to present us with a Middle-earth equivalent of our Carboniferous and Cretaceous, with its dinosaurs and gymnosperm plants. The only inconsistency is the reference to the "grasses" for even these are flowering plants, though they may not look like flowers. We even have a Cretaceous/Tertiary or K/T boundary in the form of the fall of Illuin and Ormal.

After the Fall of the Lamps, we are told that Yavanna set a Sleep upon the blighted land and only the fell creatures of

Melkor would seem then to thrive, for Oromë would, at regular intervals, come to Middle-earth and hunt them. Thus, when the Elves awoke, where did they obtain their food and clothing from? One may admit that, being as yet unfallen creatures, they may not find the need to cover themselves until much later, but the matter of their food is much more complex: the world they appear into does not seem very conducive to feeding them. I know little about the eating qualities of bracken, save that they may be edible when their fronds are very young, but even sheep avoid it. A flowerless world is a fruitless world, and all the roots and tubers we know are of flowering plants. I lose myself in conjectures and would welcome your comments.

In like manner to this, the whole civilisation of the Elves in Valinor appears blurred and unfocused, deliberately so, I think, for fear of revealing the raw material beneath and because of Tolkien's own argument as expressed above. It is not wise to assess an earthly paradise made for Elves with a Mannish yardstick. It is fine to do so with Middle-earth, because, in the end, it is our own world we see reflected back at us, but Aman is different in essence and its magic falls apart when viewed through a Mannish magnifying-glass. However, there may be many people who would wish to do so, and they do it at their own risk. In so doing, they, we, I, may all be walking a tightrope, which is fine as long as we are aware of it, but woe betide whoever falls from this narrow ledge, for there may not be a lack of eager lions who would rend their arguments to pieces! We must remember that human utopias never work, for they always have a flaw at heart which brings about their downfall. Valinor may work as an Elven utopia, but not as a Mannish one: let us leave it as it is, or, if not, treat it with utmost care and consideration. In looking too closely at this description of the distant past, we might come to see the seams of the story, and thus to undermine our confidence in the whole edifice.

It is my belief that in order to take all of Tolkien's world in and survive at this level of study, we need to be of two minds at once, like somebody who could hold in his mind at once the attitudes of a Bishop of Durham and of a Mid-Western religious fundamentalist, of a neo-Darwinist and a creationist. Tolkien himself was very scientifically-minded and yet was a devout Catholic: he kept rewriting his Mythology in order to keep up with the scientific advancements of the time. It was not his fault that science in this century has progressed more rapidly than even he could do to keep up with it!

Thus it seems that the only way we can accept his conception of the early days of Arda and of its dwellers is to acknowledge its *Big Time* qualities.

Purity and Danger in Middle-earth

By Chris Seeman

This paper is about evil in Middle-earth. It is derivative of a broader interest in Tolkien's overall discourse of power, a topic which is currently taking on the contours of a thesis-length project. It also follows from another paper delivered at the Arda Symposium on Evil in Tolkien's writing, in which I explored the relationship between moral evil and the cosmology of the secondary world. In it I chose to embrace a distinction between the moral and descriptive dimensions of evil (cf. Parkin, 1985, 7). In this very general sense evil may be said to have two faces (which may or may not be causally related). The first of these might be thought of as sin or deviance, which contains within it the moral evaluation of an action. In the secondary world Tolkien conceives of such evil as a process of Fall or moral degeneration, generated by conditions which often inhere in the nature of the created order itself. So, for example, the downfall of Númenor is partly a consequence of its proximity to the Blessed Realm and the inevitable sense of privation generated by that proximity. Similarly the corruption of the Elven-smiths of Eregion proceeds from the spiral of diminishment to which they are subject by virtue of their very presence in Middle-earth following the changing of the world.

Both of these examples point to the fact that there are two

kinds of evil in Middle-earth: there is moral evil, and there is the set of largely unintentional conditions which are conducive of, and which may lead to, such moral evil. But suffering and misfortune are not merely *causes* of evil, for sin and deviance inevitably produce outcomes. The majority of suffering in Middle-earth has a personal (and, hence, morally discernible) cause. This generally holds even when no immediate source of deviance is evident. The many hapless chances that befall Túrin, for example, are not chances at all but are instead caused by the malevolent will of Morgoth in Angband. On the other hand while the statement "the hour is evil, for Angband's Shadow lies heavily upon it" contains an implicit moral evaluation of Angband, it does not imply that the hour itself is morally reprehensible; it remains essentially a descriptive statement. Suffering and misfortune may, therefore, be said to constitute a descriptive dimension of evil – descriptive not merely by virtue of its indicative mode but because the dominant idioms and metaphors which constitute it may express something about the nature of evil and its relationship to how power is conceptualised. To say that Angband's Shadow lies heavily upon this hour and that is why its evil does not, of course, indicate that the peaks of Thangorodrim cast shadows upon intervals of time – rather it constructs the idiom of Shadow (and, by implication, light and darkness) as a discourse of power. How, then, does Tolkien narrate the outcomes of evil and what does this tell us about the secondary world and the operations of power within it?

Power, of course, is a very slippery concept and may prove difficult to define in formal terms without rendering it inoperative for analytic purposes. As a quality or property, the *Oxford English Dictionary* defines power as the "ability to do or to effect something or anything" (vol. 2, 2263). So much for abstraction. Tolkien himself makes use of the term in several contexts, often pejorative though not always so. But the definitional elusivity of power is not the result of any necessary lack of clarity, but instead follows from the fact that it is not a discrete domain of reference, abstracted or divorced from a larger perspective about the nature of the world and the nature of action within the world, which is known as cosmology.

In her seminal work, *Purity and Danger*, the anthropologist Mary Douglas has argued that idioms of pollution and their presumed outcomes on both the physical and social bodies serve to demarcate cosmology. Her proposal derives from the old adage that dirt is essentially matter out of place (Dougas, 1966, 2). Disorder presumes an ordered system of which it is a contravention, and so the discourse of pollution (and its opposite purity) reveals implicit patterns of organising the world and of conceptualising the nature of power within it. The *instrumental* effects or outcomes of evil in Middle-earth are, therefore, simultaneously expressive of the world in which they subsist.[1]

---

1. For the dual nature of pollution discourse (cf. Douglas, 1966, 3) Douglas's presentation of what she variously calls the creative, expressive, or communicative function of pollution beliefs is somewhat skewed by her Durkheimian perspective that cosmology is a one-to-one "reflection" of social reality, and while she admits on occasion that the relationship between ideas and practices is not so simple as this (Douglas, 1966, 4) in practice she fails to treat pollution concepts as *ideology* which displaces or "refracts" rather than simply reflects or mirrors actual practice. This is a highly salient distinction, particularly if one wishes to examine the relationship between the secondary world and Tolkien's own views which control the ideological "shape" of that world. This, however, is a different task from that of the present paper.

"The idiom of pollution", writes Douglas, "lends itself to a complex algebra which takes into account the variables in each context" (Douglas, 1966, 9). In *The Silmarillion* we are told that Varda hallowed the Silmarils "so that thereafter no mortal flesh, nor hands unclean, nor anything of evil will might touch them but it was scorched and withered" (Tolkien, 1977, 77). To be hallowed is to be set apart, and to be set apart is to be charged with power. Varda's hallowing of the jewels has the instrumental goal of protecting them from polluting evil, such that bodily contact with the Silmarils is itself polluting. Morgoth's hands are burned black by their touch, "and black they remained ever after; nor was he ever free from the pain of the burning, and the anger of the pain" (Tolkien, 1977, 93). Similarly, both Maedhros and Maglor find the jewels' touch unbearable because of their evil actions. By contrast Beren's hand is not burnt, mortal though he is.

The expressive function of pollution to which Douglas has previously alluded may be seen to be operative in the above examples in more than one way. Bodily contact with the holy jewels serves to locate a person *horizontally* on the moral map of Middle-earth, Morgoth being the more obvious example. The case of the sons of Fëanor is highly significant in the context of the directly preceding scene in which Maglor and Maedhros debate whether they have a just claim on the Silmarils, given Manwë's revocation of their Oath (Tolkien, 1977, 287). One of the functions of pollution according to Douglas is to determine innocence or guilt in morally ambiguous situation. Moral judgment is made post hoc according to the simple criterion of whether pollution is present or not (Douglas, 1966, 131). So we are told that when the jewel burned his hand Maedhros perceived "that it was as Eönwë had said, and that his right thereto had become void, and that the oath was vain" (Tolkien, 1977, 288).

But whereas pollution from contact with the Silmaril locates them horizontally outside the moral pale, the case of Beren points to the way the *absence* of pollution can indicate *vertical* distinctions in the cosmic order. The reason for the danger present in the Silmarils for mortal flesh but not for Elves or Valar is not made clear. It appears to relate to the concept of magnitude: that power exists in a hierarchy of intensities, and that one's relative position on this ladder determines whether or not contact with a powerful object will be corrosive to one's being. In Middle-earth this hierarchy of intensity seems to be primarily determined by what Tolkien sometimes called a given race's "biological and spiritual nature". Pollution illuminates the principles by which power is organised. In the case of the Silmarils vertical classification is defined primarily by the *temporal* relationship of the actor to the created order. The Silmaril that Lúthien wore as a mortal woman hastened her death because "it was too bright for mortal lands" (Tolkien, 1977, 268). Here again we note the intersection of pollution discourse with the idiom of *light*. Another example of this is the reply which the Eldar make to the Númenórean desire for immortality:

"little would it profit you. For it is not the land of Manwë that makes its people deathless, but the Deathless that dwell therein have hallowed the land; and there you would but wither and grow weary the sooner, as moths in a light too strong and steadfast." (Tolkien, 1977, 299).

The temporal principle of vertical classification in Middle-earth, I would suggest, corresponds to the following temporal relationships to the world: mortality, Elvish longevity (coeval with the life of the Earth), immortality (for the Ainur who dwell in the world but are not of it, who existed before it and had a part in its making), and Divinity (being the source of all power and, hence, not bounded by it). According to this scheme Beren would be considered an anomaly because he is mortal and yet not harmed by contact with the light of the jewel. The absence of pollution sets him apart from his mortal classification and elevates him above his limits. He is therefore a limit-breaking agent.

The liminal status of Beren is manifested in other parts of the story as well. Early on he passes the Girdle of Melian, a purity boundary which has no power to restrain him as Melian had, herself, prophesied: "doom greater than my power shall send him, and the songs that shall spring from that coming shall endure when all Middle-earth is changed" (Tolkien, 1977, 164). In this prophecy we learn that doom or fate is the agency controlling Beren's anomalous vertical status, or "the finger of God" as Tolkien sometimes called it. It is presumably this divine grace which accounts for the preservation of Beren's hand incorrupt within the belly of the wolf. The absence of pollution from contact with the Silmaril is therefore one of the principal means by which Beren's status and identity is produced.

The foregoing discussion would seem to support Douglas's contention that dirt is matter out of place, that descriptive evil represents the intersection of vertical and horizontal modes of organising the secondary world. The validity of her thesis must rest on its ability to incorporate and to interpret all instances of descriptive evil in terms of her categories. Douglas argues that there are four basic type of pollution (Douglas, 1966, 122):

1. Pollution which attacks external boundaries. Examples of this would include Beren and Carcharoth's crossing of the Girdle of Melian into Doriath, Melkor's assault upon Arda from the void, and his later penetration of the fences of Aman with Ungoliant.

2. Pollution generated by the transgression of the internal categories of the created order. This is most frequently incurred by perceived moral deviance, including the act of mixing categories which should not be mixed (such as the marriage of Human and Elf). Melkor's discord and his desire to possess the secret fire would be an example of this, as would the revolt of Ar-Pharazôn against the Ban of the Valar. The later example is particularly significant because it results in the reordering of creation in the Akallabêth.

3. Pollution which is generated by and inheres in boundaries and margins. Hence, bodily contact with the Silmarils, or proximity to Sauron whose touch misshapes whatever it comes into contact with (Tolkien, 1977, 177). Númenor's proximity to Aman is also simultaneously a source of power and of constant danger. Note, however, that contact with margins is different from something like Carcharoth's swallowing of the Silmaril which would instead be a transgression of internal boundaries – a mixing of opposing categories.

4. Pollution which inheres in the contradictions of the created order itself. This aspect of pollution is important for understanding descriptive evil, since evil in Middle-earth is inherently contradictory. Melkor's

discord, for example, is self-defeating because its hubristic motivation leads only to his more complete subordination to the designs of Eru. Similarly the oath of Fëanor, which has the purpose of restoring to the Noldor what is rightfully theirs, will lead only to their self-destruction: "It will drive them, and yet betray them, and ever snatch away the treasures that they have sworn to pursue. To evil end shall all things turn that they begin" (Tolkien, 1977, 100).

Thus for Douglas's model of pollution as a contravention of order would seem to be compatible with Tolkien's narration of evil in the secondary world, but can it account for all manifestations of evil in Middle-earth? Her proposal has the weakness of being biased by her Durkheimian perspective that evil is essentially the violation of moral norms. Pollution and evil are for her, relative concepts: "There is no such thing as absolute dirt: it exists in the eye of the beholder" (Douglas, 1966, 2). At first glance this might appear to correlate with Tolkien's own views expressed in his letters, in which he writes "I do not think that there is such a thing [as Absolute evil], since that is zero. I do not believe at any rate that any rational being is wholly evil" (Tolkien, 1981, 243). Tolkien makes this point to clarify his view that evil must always involve a process of Fall and that it does not therefore exist *ex nihilo*. Granting this, the fact remains that radical or absolute evil *does* appear (in derivative form) in "The Darkening of Valinor". The Unlight of Ungoliant is more than a mere absence of light: "In that hour was made a Darkness that seemed not lack but a thing with being of its own: For it was indeed made by malice out of Light, and it had the power to pierce the eye, and to enter heart and mind, and strangle the very will" (Tolkien, 1977, 87-8). In a collection of essays entitled *The Anthropology of Evil*, David Parkin identifies a distinction between what he calls the strong and weak senses of moral evil (Parkin, 1985, 5). "Weak evil" refers to the Durkheimian view (largely embraced by Douglas) that evil is a contravention of ethical rules. Weak evil is simply a by-product of a coherent and ordered universe. By contrast, "Strong evil" implies that evil is in some sense self-generating and *sui generis* rather than derivative of order in some essential way. While Tolkien's own claim that absolute, non-derivative evil does not appear in his stories is correct, the presence of Unlight seems to be much closer to the Strong that the Weak pole of evil, and so may be partially explained in those terms. The other main example of this kind of evil is Melkor's initial rebellion, which does not *explicitly* derive its meaning from any created order as such (since it occurs before that order comes into existence and in fact has an irreversible impact on the nature of that creation).

These two problematic areas draw attention to one of the inherent limitations of Douglas's approach: namely that it is incapable of conceiving pollution as *process* but must view it instead in terms of pseudo-structuralist categories ("boundaries" and "classifications" which are more or less static). Both the discord of Melkor and the Unlight of Ungoliant *involve* a system of classification but they can only be understood as primarily concerned with the *transformation* of categories through personal agency. Melkor, for example, significantly goes out into the void (a potential place of disorder) before initiating his revolt, but the desire for the Secret Fire in the first place is unexplained – it simply happens in a self-generating fashion. Similarly, Ungoliant dwells in the region of Avathar "where the shadows were deepest and thickest in the world" (Tolkien, 1977, 84) but the source of her corruption is Melkor rather than her location in the cosmos (which itself seems to be less causal than expressive). Moreover, it is her own malice which transforms the self-generating Light of the Trees into a self-generating Unlight. Douglas by contrast contends that pollution resides not in *persons* but in *structures* (of course by persons she means primarily humans rather than gods, but Tolkien's own perspective in *The Silmarillion* must be taken into consideration – it is not primarily "about" humans but is rather written *from the perspective of Elves and Valar*). Douglas's framework may therefore productively contribute to the development of an understanding of Tolkien's conception of power but cannot, by itself, adequately explain the narration of it in its totality.

To sum up briefly thus far, Douglas's model of pollution or descriptive evil as expressive of ordering, cosmological principles may be used as an heuristic perspective for examining how power is classified, both horizontally in terms of morality and vertically in terms of intensity and magnitude. The latter mode of classification also draws our attention to the role of *time* as medium for relating persons to the hierarchy of power. Pollution may result from the crossing of external boundaries, the mixing of internal lines, contact or proximity with margins, and contradictions inhering in the created order itself. A final significant aspect of pollution is that it invariably involves a discourse of the body. For Douglas the human body serves as a model for any bounded system (such as a social or cosmic order) – the various kinds of pollution concern (over external boundaries, internal classifications, margins, and so forth) are for her symbolised by bodily boundaries, margins, and orifices (Douglas, 1966, 115). The make-up of personhood is of fundamental interest because categories such as body and soul or body and mind often mediate conceptions of power. Moreover, an attention to the process by which the person is corrupted or deconstructed by polluting agency not only tells us something of Tolkien's own understanding of the person, but also may reveal something more specific about the nature of pollution as *process* (rather than as matter statically out of *place*).

In the above quoted passage, the Unlight of Ungoliant is said to "pierce the eye, and enter heart and mind, and strangle the very will." This is significant for our purposes not only in that it provides a classification of the type of polluting operations involved with evil, but that it is suggestive of the domains of a person's being which may be affected, perhaps even as a progressive movement from the eyes as orifices or margins, into the heart and mind as a transgressive attack on external boundaries, and strangling the very will as a distortive violation of internal categories. Before testing this hypothesis out on the many examples found in *The Silmarillion* and *Unfinished Tales*, a tentative model of the body must be articulated on the basis of evidence in the narrative.

We are already given two significant linguistic clues from the Appendices of *The Lord of the Rings* (Tolkien, 1966c, 401): the Quenya terms *óre* and *thúle*. Óre is translated as "heart or inner mind", suggesting that the aforementioned passage of Unlight entering heart and mind may refer to a unified domain. Thúle is glossed in English as "spirit" and many instances of semantic association suggest that thúle is closely related if not identical in conception to "will". Be that as it may, Tolkien's actual usage is not always consistent. In one of the letters

47

in which Sauron's diminishment is discussed, he formally equates spirit and will, which he then goes on to define as "the effective link between the indestructible mind and being, and the realisation of its imagination" (Tolkien, 1981, 260). In the context of the discussion the somewhat abstract "realisation of the imagination" most likely refers to the physical body as he is speaking about Sauron's status as a Maia. I would venture to suggest as a general rule that Tolkien conceives of will as the active dimension of the broader principle of spirit, which seems to occupy a more passive role as potential energy.

A final preliminary clue to Tolkien's anthropology deriving from the letters is his frequent use of the phrase "rational incarnate being" to refer to mortals, Elves, and Ainur. "Rational" might be broadly correlative to óre in in its aspect of "mind", while "being" may be identified with thúle because it is always by means of the Flame Imperishable (the Spirit) that Eru gives *being* to an act of sub-creation.[2] "Incarnate" would of course refer to physical embodiment, and finally "will" would constitute the active operations of óre and thúle upon the physical body and the physical world. We should therefore take óre, thúle, will, and body as the four principal components of a rudimentary anthropology for the purpose of exploring the kinds of effects pollution may have on a character in the secondary world. First, however, it will be necessary to investigate Tolkien's actual usage of these concepts in more detail.

Óre as heart or inner mind embraces a wide variety of associations for Tolkien. It may refer to intention, or to

---

2. I tentatively embrace the view put forth by Paul Kocher that the Secret Fire is vaguely equivalent to the Holy Spirit (cf. Kocher, 1985).

perception; to intelligence, consciousness, rationality, and the capacity to communicate. Óre also involves the sub-creative faculty of imagination and mental power in general. Tolkien conceives of óre as indestructible (even by the Creator) but breakable by force: the heart may be corrupted and the mind overthrown. Thúle or spirit, then, is closely related to the sub-creative dimension of óre. Like óre, it is conferred directly by the creator and is indestructible, begotten not made, the essence of one's being. Nevertheless, spirit can also be broken, diminished, spent, exhausted, enhanced, or enlarged. Significant to this last type of modification is that on two occasions Tolkien identifies this "spiritual enlargement" with the notion of "sanctification" (Tolkien, 1981, 203, 331) which is an explicit term for purity and so is directly linked up to the discourse of power. It also indicates that it is vulnerable to pollution.

Together, then, óre and thúle make up the unity "rational being". The physical body completes the person by its incarnation. For the Ainur who are not by nature incarnate, the body is a realisation of the óre, but even for Elves and Mortals the body is merely the house of the spirit, hence the body forms the visible expression of the relative state of purity or corruption inherent to that person's spirit. The will might be said to be the connecting relationship between óre and thúle on the one hand and their visible manifestation on the other. The two main orifices or channels of the will are the eyes and mouth; these are the margins of the body which are vulnerable to pollution. This is one of the reasons for the fact that most prevalent form of pollution in Middle-earth is the distortion of perceptions (through either the visual or aural faculties). Unlike the óre and thúle, the will which links perception to a person's essential being may be totally annihilated or controlled by a hostile force.

Destructive power may have one of three different outcomes on the person: it can destroy or corrupt the physical body, it can dominate or pervert the will (and by implication the óre and thúle), and it can distort perceptions or contaminate the senses. As the body is the expression of óre and thúle, so agents of pollution can often be identified by their bodily appearance and physical presence: Morgoth and seemingly all of his servants have black blood, revealing their corrupt insides; Glaurung exudes slime and filth wherever he goes, defiling all in his wake (Tolkien, 1980a, 119, 134). So too his stench is so foul that horses are driven to madness by its presence (Tolkien, 1980a, 127, 133, 134; Tolkien, 1977, 248). Also the mere proximity of Ungoliant and her brood poisons the waters of Ered Gorgoroth (Tolkien, 1977, 139). The blight of Melkor's hatred physically mars the Spring of Arda so that "Green things fell sick and rotted, and rivers were chocked with weeds and slime, and fens were made rank and poisonous, the breeding place of flies..." (Tolkien, 1977, 41).

The will may be dominated principally through the orifice or margin of the eyes. Glaurung is able to halt Túrin moveless with his gaze and hold his will in subjection (Tolkien, 1977, 243). Captives brought to Angband are so daunted by Morgoth's eyes "that they needed chain no more, but walked ever in fear of him, doing his will wherever they might" (Tolkien, 1977, 132). But it is sensual perception itself which is most vulnerable to polluting agency – its corruption is most pronounced because perception causes characters to evaluate and take action which can be as self-destructive as it is destructive towards others in turn. It is fitting, therefore, that the eyes should symbolise the danger that they do. "I am blind!" cries Túrin in his despair,

"Groping since childhood in a dark mist of Morgoth!" (Tolkien, 1980a, 194).

Morgoth's penultimate act of perceptual pollution is his filling of darkness with fear for all living things and of confounding that fear with perceptions about death (Tolkien, 1977, 34, 47). Here again we find that this astigmation inheres in the very structure of the created order, but it is not really a matter of "place" (as Douglas would argue) as it is a matter of corruption – a distortive displacement of perception by the act of some person. The control which Melkor is able to exercise by the power of his will in the reordering of perception is most clearly seen in the darkening of Valinor:

> "amid his fair words others were woven, so subtly that many who heard them believed in recollection that they arose from their own thought... and then whispers went abroad that the Valar had brought the Eldar to Aman because of their jealousy... But Melkor spoke to them in secret of Mortal Men, seeing how the silence of the Valar might be twisted to evil... the peace of Valinor was poisoned... and many became filled with pride, forgetting how much of what they had and knew came to them in gift from the Valar" (Tolkien, 1977, 68, 69).

Even when the lies of Melor are revealed, their reversal still has an irrevocable distortive impact on perception. Because of the exile of Fëanor "the lies of Melkor were made true in seeming, though Fëanor by his own deeds had brought this thing to pass; and the bitterness that Melkor had sown endured" (Tolkien, 1977, 81, 82). Similarly, even though Fëanor utterly rejected Melkor at Formenos, his words concerning the Valar irresistibly pollute his perceptions in the Ring of Doom, ultimately controlling his choice of action:

> "It seemed to him that he was beset by a ring of enemies, and
> the words of Melkor returned to him, saying that the Silmarils
> were not safe, if the Valar would possess them. 'And is he not
> Vala as are they', said his thought, 'and does he not understand
> their hearts? Yea, a thief shall reveal thieves!'" (Tolkien, 1977,
> 90).

In Beleriand Morgoth is able to poison the hearts of the
Eldar with fear and despair through the work of his spies, who
mingle lies with the truth concerning the Noldor so that the
Eldar become estranged from them (Tolkien, 1977, 178). He
is also able to use the will of his own vision to twist the fate of
Húrin's son:

> "all that Morgoth knew of the working of his malice Húrin
> knew also, but lies were mingled with the truth, and aught
> that was good was hidden or distorted. In all ways Morgoth
> sought most to cast an evil light on those things that Thingol
> and Melian had done" (Tolkien, 1977, 258).

But at the words of Melian this distortion is revealed:

> "Húrin Thalion, Morgoth hath bewitched thee; for he that
> seeth through Morgoth's eyes, willing or unwilling, seeth
> all things crooked... With the voice of Morgoth thou dost
> now upbraid thy friends... And hearing the words of Melian
> Húrin stood moveless, and he gazed long into the eyes of the
> Queen; and there in Menegroth, defended still by the Girdle
> of Melian from the darkness of the Enemy, he read the truth
> of all that was done, and tasted at last the fullness of woe that

was measured for him by Morgoth Bauglir... 'now my Fate is fulfilled, and the purpose of Morgoth achieved; but I am his thrall no longer'" (Tolkien, 1977,263).

The pollution of perception is relative to the eye of the beholder for Douglas because it cannot be conjured out of nothing. The will of Morgoth modifies, distorts, or displaces already existing perceptions but he cannot create pure illusion. So too in the later part of the Third Age Sauron's possession of the Palantír allows him to use it as a channel of will to dominate Denethor's perception, by selectively revealing and concealing facts so as to reconstitute them or re-present them in such a way that their totality (or the illusion of their totality) produces a distortion.

The foregoing has been an attempt to explore the applicability of Douglas's work for an understanding of Tolkien's world: that the idiom of purity and pollution contains within it implicit meanings which express the relationship between power and principles of cosmology, that pollution may be viewed in terms of process or as matter out of place, and that an understanding of Tolkien's anthropology of the body can provide suggestive insights into the more specific forms of pollution upon the person. The value in exploring the descriptive dimension of evil in Tolkien's work is that while dirt or pollution is always a negative category, the act of identifying it implies a creative reordering of the world. The discourse of evil contains within it the discourse of power in general, and so an understanding of evil in its many facets is an essential first step to outlining the contours of Tolkien's conception and imagination of power and its integral role in the sub-creative process of inventing a secondary world.

A final word about the categories of pollution and purity in relation to power. Both imply an *aesthetic* mode of representation, which constructs good and evil as something immediate to sensory perception. In his book, *The Ideology of the Aesthetic*, Terry Eagleton has identified several points of intersection between aesthetic cognition and conception of power (Eagleton, 1990). The aesthetic practice of sub-creation (and its Tolkienian antithesis of domination) are both represented by Tolkien in his works by the polluting or sanctificatory outcomes of power. It is in his essay "On Faery Stories" (Tolkien, 1964) that this intersection of aesthetic production and its narrative representation is articulated, and it is this which shall become the focus of my thesis. Douglas's work on pollution and her subsequent work on cosmology contributes to this project in clarifying how Tolkien works out an aesthetic within his literary corpus in the details of the substantive narrative text.

"Good People": Elves of the First Age

By Alex Lewis

I wish to examine the differences between the Elves of the First Age and those of the Second Age and the Third Age. When I began the examination, I discovered that it became a discussion of the nature of Elves and their "humanisation" at closer quarters, as viewed in *The Silmarillion*, as opposed to their "remoteness" in *The Lord of the Rings* and *The Hobbit*.

For Elves of the Second and Third Ages probably received better "press" than those of earlier times. The tales we follow in the Second and Third Ages are tales about Men with Elves coming into them obliquely as observers, principally, and not, as is the case in the First Age, about Elves with Men being the "second comers".

Elves, as Tolkien said, (1978, 145) are "Good People", by which we are led to believe that they are inherently good and think no evil thoughts and do no evil deeds. In *The Hobbit* there is a slight deviation from this "goodness" only in one isolated case – that of Thranduil the Elven King who imprisoned Thorin and company with very little cause and was actually willing to do battle with the Dwarves to gain the treasure of Erebor, to which he had no legitimate claim whatsoever (Tolkien, 1978, 215). Yet even he stayed his march and gave aid to the Laketowners when asked before heading on to the

Lonely Mountain – a delay that in all probability cost him the ownership of the treasure in the end (Tolkien, 1978, 220). But other than this one case – and these Woodland Elves are said to be less wise than the Deep-Elves, and so perhaps their origin excuses them somewhat for their actions – all other Elves act in a manner befitting the title "Good People". The Last Homely House is a model for charity and goodwill to all with no thought of gain (Tolkien, 1978, 50). From the pages of *The Lord of the Rings*, we are used to descriptions of the Elves as "wonderful folk" or "wondrous folk", held in awe and admiration by Sam Gamgee and to a slightly lesser degree by Frodo.

But the descriptions we have of Elves of the Third Age come from the pens of Frodo and Sam, both of whom cared little of the earlier ages (Tolkien, 1966a, 23-25). For Frodo and Sam did not read much of Bilbo's Translations from the Elvish which Christopher Tolkien states to have been *The Silmarillion* (Tolkien, 1983). They did not speak much with Elrond concerning the Elder Days. We meet Elves such as Gildor Inglorion and his company in the woods near Pincup (Tolkien, 1966a, 89) and their open-handedness and generosity is evident; these beings would offer harm to no living creature and would only fight to defend themselves. They take Frodo and his companions into their fold and protect them from the Black Riders and feed them too.

Glorfindel is a shining white lord who is full of concern for Frodo's plight and his wounding when he meets Strider and the Hobbits on the road to Rivendell; he puts Frodo on his own horse and saves Frodo from the Black Riders in doing so (Tolkien, 1966a, 223-6). The Elf we know most about through the pages of *The Lord of the Rings* is a being called Legolas Greenleaf, son of Thranduil the King of the woodland Elves who was the anomaly in *The Hobbit* (Tolkien, 1966a, 253). Legolas has more than just concern for the environment, he senses its distress in a personal way. He listens to the voices of the stones lamenting in Eregion – "deep they delved us, fair they wrought us, high they builded us; but they are gone." (Tolkien, 1966a, 297). He feels the goodness in the Mallorn trees in Lórien (Tolkien, 1966a, 352) and when meeting Fangorn, he gains what few others do: permission to visit his forest and take with him a Dwarf (Tolkien, 1966c, 259 and 1966b, 191). He needs no sleep; wrapping himself in waking memories instead and will offer harm to nothing, other than Orcs, which are inferred to be "beyond hope of salvation; twisted wicked creatures", and therefore fair game for slaughtering. This very subject of the Orcs unredeemable wickedness seems to have caused Tolkien a great deal of thought over the years.

The Elves' position as stated by Elrond – himself a paragon of virtue, wisdom and goodness – in both *The Lord of the Rings* and *The Hobbit* is of pacifistic benign onlookers who have much wisdom born of their long years. They would willingly give up Middle-earth to the Men that will follow them and go West, lose even their three rings (Tolkien, 1966a, 282) if it means getting rid of Sauron once and for all. In *The Lord of the Rings*, even Thranduil's mistrust of strangers and his maltreatment of the Dwarves comes through as being mistrust born of wickedness that he has seen perpetrated by others against Elves, and Gandalf is very quick to paper over the cracks when Glóin brings the matter up at the Council of Elrond (Tolkien, 1966a, 268) when reference is made to Gollum's escape from Thranduil's Halls.

The female Elves we meet, such as Galadriel and Arwen, are also very neutral in their political approach and they help their guests – giving gifts of great worth and significance, in

Arwen's case the white gem to Frodo (Tolkien, 1966c, 253), and in Galadriel's case a whole host of gifts to the Fellowship (Tolkien, 1966a, 391-3).

If one examines the Tale of Years for the Third Age and compares it to that for the Second Age, Elves are mentioned (Tolkien, 1966c, 363-75) much less in the Third than in the Second – 14 out of 36 entries for the Second Age (or 39%) and 12 out of 129 entries for the Third Age (or 9%).

So, uncovered and thrust into the spotlight through the pages of *The Silmarillion*, what sort of beings were the Elves of the First Age? Christopher Tolkien is careful to point out (Tolkien, 1977, 344) in his definition of "Noldor" that it means knowledgeable and not wise. The First Age began with the appearance of the Sun and the Moon, but already the Noldor's hands were sullied with blood; the Kinslaying was behind them (Tolkien, 1977, 87), and it was not only the Fëanorians who slew the Teleri at Alqualondë. Yet before this the Noldor had manufactured weaponry, and Fëanor had drawn his sword against his half brother Fingolfin (Tolkien, 1977, 70) and been banished by the Valar from Tirion. Finwë, Fëanor's father, would not come to Tirion for favour towards and love of his eldest son, and Fëanor left the Silmarils behind and deprived the Elves and Valar their sight (Tolkien, 1977, 75), thus leading to his father's death at the hands of Melkor and the theft of the jewels he so coveted.

Their motives were very human ones: pride, greed and fear. Pride of the father who felt unkinged, greed of the son who desired his own creations beyond the bonds of blood, fear of the son who felt threatened by his half-brothers gaining favour with their father, and fear of all the Noldor of the Second-comers – due to the whisperings of Melkor in their ears. This led Fëanor and his seven sons to swear their terrible Oath (Tolkien, 1977,

83) with pride and their hatred for Melkor. Whether their hatred and their war was just or no, these Elves were far removed from the pacifist non-active Elves of the Third Age. Perhaps the Third Age Elves had seen too many defeats and too much sorrow and were weary of Middle-earth.

The perspective of distance and remoteness present in the history that underpins *The Lord of the Rings* is removed in *The Silmarillion*, for it is the history *in itself*, and as Tolkien himself feared (Tolkien, 1983) the magic and alienness suffered – most especially that of the Elves who were observed as being "unearthly" in the Third Age, but were reduced and became very "human" as seen close up in the pages of *The Silmarillion*. This is an inevitable process for all could not be harmony in the First and Second Ages, and yet be worth the telling.

Then even before the First Age had begun, we observe the bitter political rift between Finarfin and Fëanor which caused Finarfin to finally forsake the March (Tolkien, 1977, 88) and return in sorrow to Valinor. Soon thereafter the Fëanorians betrayed Fingolfin's folk (Tolkien, 1977, 90) and stranded them on the shores of Valinor while the White ships of the Teleri burned at Losgar.

But do not come to the conclusion that it was only the Noldor who acted in this un-goodly manner. The Elves of Beleriand in the days before the Sun and the Moon all but wiped out the race of the Petty-dwarves who had fled the Dwarf cities of Belegost and Nogrod, the founders of the caverns of Nargothrond, not knowing what manner of beast they were. Of all their people, only Mîm and his two sons lived on Amon Rûdh where they had hidden themselves cunningly and so remained untroubled by the Grey-elves of the woods (Tolkien, 1979, 204). Their names were remembered only in the ancient tales of Doriath and Nargothrond (Tolkien, 1977, 204). This is reminiscent of Legolas's rationalisation of the slaying of Orcs, though here it has a new dimension whereas Orcs were known to be wicked, the Petty-dwarves were not. It can be seen from this that the history of the Elves even before the dawning of the new sun and moon over Middle-earth was already less than laudable.

The First Age was an age typified by mistrust and plotting amongst the Princes of Beleriand. Thingol of Doriath (Tolkien, 1977, 111) was extremely unhappy to find that the Noldor had arrived in Middle-earth, even though their arrival had pushed back Melkor's Orcs. Only Elves of Finarfin's House were allowed into his realm. The Mereth Aderthad (Tolkien, 1977, 113), a Feast of Reuniting, was surely an event that any who wished to mediate and be seen as reasonable would have attended, a sort of League of Nations of Beleriand. Not King Thingol. He sent two messengers. Striving for power was rife; for instance, when Angrod spoke to Thingol about where the Noldor might live within Beleriand, Caranthir – who is described as being the harshest and quickest to anger of all the sons of Fëanor – rebuked him and was angry with him (Tolkien, 1977, 112) almost causing a permanent rift between the Princes of Beleriand. Only the skilful intervention of Maedhros prevented a lot more damage. When Thingol learned the truth about the Kinslaying, his reaction was to ban the use of Quenya the language of Valinor (Tolkien, 1977, 129). This seems strange when his wife was Melian, one of the Maia, and was herself of Valinor of old.

Of the Grey-elves, we hear most of Eöl the Dark Elf and his son Maeglin. Eöl was haughty and proud and willing to kill his son Maeglin if he did not obey his orders, and instead killed his wife Aredhel by mistake – he used a poison tipped weapon (Tolkien, 1977, 138), something that seems extremely evil in intent; the only other time that poisoned weapons are mentioned are with the Orcs in Moria after Sam was cut on the forehead (Tolkien, 1966a, 350) and with Celebrían, Elrond's wife, when she was captured by the Orcs of the Misty Mountains (Tolkien, 1966c, 323). Maeglin was a son who took after his father, and he brought about by betrayal to Morgoth the Fall of Gondolin (Tolkien, 1977, 242) and at the height of the battle for the city, he tried to seize Idril by force and to kill Eärendil by casting him into the flames (Tolkien, 1977, 242).

In their dealings with Men, Elves of the First Age were very changeable and perhaps even manipulative. Finrod Felagund, known amongst Bëor's people as Nóm, (Tolkien, 1977, 141) was extremely welcoming and did not seek to make use of them. Fingolfin also was pleased to see them and as High King of the Noldor took them into his service (Tolkien, 1977, 143). The Green Elves of Beleriand were very unfriendly towards them and asked Finrod to make them go back to where they had come from to the East of the Mountains or else they would hunt them and slay them for cutting trees and disturbing their lands (Tolkien, 1977, 142). It is said that of the sons of Fëanor, Caranthir in Thargelion paid little heed to Men (Tolkien, 1977, 143), but that after the people of Haldad were attacked by Orcs, he looked kindly on them and offered Haldad's daughter his protection, though it was refused (Tolkien, 1977, 145). Maedhros – eldest son of Fëanor – also seems to have been well disposed to the newly arrived Men and many took service with him (Tolkien, 1977, 145). Thingol was for long very cool towards Men and forbade any to cross his borders even though Melian knew full well that they would play an important part in the fate of Beleriand. When one did, Thingol treated Beren, the son of Barahir, very unfairly indeed and set him a task to win the hand of his daughter which he thought would be his death (Tolkien, 1977, 167). This was strange considering that Thingol himself had aspired to wed Melian, a Maia of Valinor, and a far greater being than he was (Tolkien, 1977, 55), and that was all that Beren was desiring, but on a lesser scale (Tolkien, 1977, 166).[1] When his daughter Lúthien tried to aid Beren, and he saw that indeed she loved him, he imprisoned her upon a beech tree known as Hírilorn, though she managed to escape her uniquely Elvish prison (Tolkien, 1977, 172).

Later, Thingol repented his harshness, though it took the loss of Beren's hand to bring it about. Thereafter, he seemed to treat Men with less contempt, even taking in the son of Húrin, Túrin Turambar, and looking after his mother and sister though it did not benefit him directly (Tolkien, 1977, 199). Yet even so, his interest in Men was bound up in the good of Doriath rather than any pure selfless act. In the end, his greed was the cause of his death, for he did not understand Dwarves and their nature and so he was slain deep in his own caverns and the Silmaril was taken away from him by force (Tolkien, 1977, 233).

Turgon in Gondolin also refused to let Men into his land at first, but unlike Thingol, he listened to wisdom and allowed first Huor and Húrin to be brought to his land and allowed them to leave – something that was previously forbidden to all, and so stirred resentment in Maeglin on account of the treatment of his father Eöl (Tolkien, 1977, 138). Then he allowed Tuor to enter his city and also was foresighted enough to allow his daughter Idril to marry Tuor who was a mortal (Tolkien, 1977, 241).

The sons of Fëanor seem at times to act like ruthless

1. I am grateful to Sysanne Stopfel for raising the interesting comparison of Thingol and Beren during a conversation.

criminals rather than "good people". Celegorm and Curufin caused in effect the death of Finrod Felagund by conspiring to turn his people against him, and so Orodreth, the brother of Finrod, banished them from Nargothrond (Tolkien, 1977, 176). The people of Nargothrond were so incensed by the way the sons of Fëanor had used and manipulated them against their king, effectively usurping his power, that they wished to execute them, but Orodreth stayed their wrath. It was at that time that Celebrimbor, the son of Curufin, forsook his father in disgust and remained behind (Tolkien, 1977, 176). The two brothers then left the caves of Nargothrond and waylaid Beren and Lúthien like a pair of common outlaws (Tolkien, 1977, 177), seeking to slay them by deception even when they owed their lives to Beren's mercy – even Huan the Hound of Valinor renounced his former master Celegorm and joined Beren and Lúthien (Tolkien, 1977, 177).

The sons of Fëanor seemed of the First Age Princes hell-bent on going down a lone path driven by their Oath. They managed to kill Dior and his wife, and to destroy Doriath and slaughter most of its people when they attempted to seize the Silmaril. Celegorm and Curufin died in that battle, though the servants of Celegorm put the sons of Dior into the woods and left them to starve to death. Maedhros, the sanest of the brothers, it seems, repented of this terrible deed and tried unsuccessfully to find them (Tolkien, 1977, 247). The sons of Fëanor then attacked the Mouths of the Sirion and the survivors of Gondolin and Doriath who lived there, trying once more to seize the Silmaril; Eärendil's two sons were captured by them (Tolkien, 1977, 247), though Maedhros treated them kindly and grew to be their friend, seeing that the violence was not doing the cause of the Fëanorians any good at all. However, Maedhros and Maglor –

the two remaining brothers – finally stooped to simple theft in the middle of the night in a desperate attempt to seize the two jewels that the hosts of Valinor had wrested from Morgoth's crown (Tolkien, 1977, 253). It is interesting that Eönwë let them go where they would, unharmed, and take with them the jewels – perhaps he saw that they had fallen beyond his aid and even that of those in the West.

Once the Oath and the theft of the Silmarils was resolved, the Elves began to settle a little better in Middle-earth. During the Second Age, they did not quarrel as much amongst themselves as far as is known, though it is interesting to note that they all lived very far from each other, Gil-galad and Círdan in Lindon at the Havens, Elrond in the Misty Mountains in Imladris and Celeborn and Galadriel in Lórien. There was some friction, perhaps between Celebrimbor and Celeborn, though what we know comes from the varied and conflicting versions in *Unfinished Tales* (Tolkien, 1980a, 228-256). It seems likely that if the story had been worked out to some consistent whole, Celebrimbor would have driven Celeborn and Galadriel from Ost-in-Edhil so making them choose Lórien as their abode. Celebrimbor and his Mírdain were driven by greed to make the Rings of Power, though whether their greed was for anything other than knowledge, it is hard to tell from the few facts we have. There seems to have been an extremely good relationship between Celebrimbor and his Dwarvish neighbours (Tolkien, 1977, 286) even though they lived on each others doorsteps.

Thereafter, the Elves only acted in combination with Men to try and overthrown Sauron. Gil-galad quickly befriended Elendil and his refugees from the Drowning of Númenor (Tolkien, 1977, 290) and aided him to establish the Northern Kingdom, building for him the towers by the sea (Tolkien,

1977, 292). It has to be said however, that by this stage there were many fewer Elves in mortal lands than during the First Age, for a great number of them had forsaken Middle-earth and returned to Valinor after the War of Wrath and the breaking of Thangorodrim (Tolkien, 1977, 286). They were a minority in Middle-earth and they knew it.

The key to the state that the Elves found themselves in during the Third Age, is given in Appendix B: "These were the fading years of the Eldar. For long they were at peace, wielding the Three Rings while Sauron slept and the One Ring was lost; but they *attempted nothing new*, living in memory of the past." (Tolkien, 1966c, 365).

It was as if the Three Rings had entrapped them in an artificial state of limbo where they were forced to be merely observers and not participants in the life and political arena of Middle-earth. In his papers, Tolkien states this quite clearly (Tolkien, 1980a, 395) and says of the Fellowship that of the Nine Walkers, Legolas achieved the least of them all.

It is as if the mere act of making the Three Rings and desiring unchange and order for all things to remain unsullied, froze the Elves in a limbo of preservation from which they were unable to break free until the One Ring was destroyed, the Three Rings lost their potency and they were able to fade gracefully from the scene of Middle-earth. Perhaps rather than being willing to sacrifice their existence in Middle-earth, they were indeed glad to find release from the bonds of mortal lands by that stage, having endured its sorrows perforce for Three long Ages.

Bibliography

Crossley-Holland, Kevin (1980), *The Norse Myths*. London: Faber and Faber.

Douglas, Mary (1966), *Purity and Danger: An Analysis of Concepts of Pollution and Taboo.* London: Routledge and Kegan Paul.

Eagleton, Terry (1990), *The Ideology of the Aesthetic*. Oxford: Basil Blackwell.

Ellison, John (1988), "Tolkien, Wagner, and the end of the Romantic Age", in (Morus et al., 1988, pp. 14-20).

Goethe, Johann Wolfgang von (1959a), translated by Philip Wayne, *Faust, Part One*. Harmondsworth: Penguin Classics.

Goethe, Johann Wolfgang von (1959b), translated by Philip Wayne, *Faust, Part Two*. Harmondsworth: Penguin Classics.

Kocher, Paul (1985), "Ilúvatar and the Secret Fire", in *Mythlore* 43, 36-37.

Mann, Thomas (1949), translated by H. T. Lowe-Porter, *Doctor Faustus*. London: Secker and Warburg.

Marlowe, Christopher (1604), *The Tragical history of Doctor Faustus*.

Morus, I. R., M. J. L. Percival and C. S. Rosenthal, eds. (1988), *Tolkien and Romanticism. Proceedings of the Cambridge Tolkien Workshop 1988*. Cambridge: Cambridge Tolkien Workshop.

Oxford English Dictionary, The (1933), Oxford: Oxford University Press.

Parkin, David, ed. (1985), *The Anthropology of Evil*. Oxford: George Allen & Unwin.

Shippey, T. A. (1982), *The Road to Middle-earth*. London: George Allen & Unwin.

Shippey, T. A. (1991), in (T. A. Shippey et al.) *Leaves from the Tree, J. R. R. Tolkien's Shorter Fiction*. London: The Tolkien Society, pp. 5-16.

Tolkien, Christopher (1983), "Foreword" in (J. R. R. Tolkien, ed. Christopher Tolkien) *The Book of Lost Tales Part I*. London: George Allen & Unwin.

Tolkien, J. R. R. (1945), "The Lay of Aotrou and Itroun", in *The Welsh Review* 4, 254-266.

Tolkien, J. R. R. (1964), "On Fairy-Stories", in (J. R. R. Tolkien) *Tree and Leaf*. London: George Allen & Unwin, pp. 9-73.

Tolkien, J. R. R. (1966a), *The Fellowship of the Ring* (second edition). London: George Allen & Unwin.

Tolkien, J. R. R. (1966b), *The Two Towers* (second edition). London: George Allen & Unwin.

Tolkien, J. R. R. (1966c), *The Return of the King* (second edition). London: George Allen & Unwin.

Tolkien, J. R. R. (1975), "The Homecoming of Beorhtnoth, Beorhthelm's Son", in (J. R. R. Tolkien) *Tree and Leaf, Smith of Wootton Major and The Homecoming of Beorhtnoth*. London: Unwin Books, pp. 147-175.

Tolkien, J. R. R. (1977) ed. Christopher Tolkien, *The Silmarillion*. London: George Allen & Unwin.

Tolkien, J. R. R. (1978), *The Hobbit* (fourth edition). London: George Allen & Unwin.

Tolkien, J. R. R. (1980a) ed. Christopher Tolkien, *Unfinished Tales*. London: George Allen & Unwin.

Tolkien, J. R. R. (1980b), "The History of Galadriel and Celeborn", in (Christopher Tolkien. ed.) *Unfinished Tales*. London: George Allen & Unwin, pp. 228-256.

Tolkien, J. R. R. (1981) ed. Humphrey Carpenter, *The Letters of J. R. R. Tolkien*. London: George Allen & Unwin.

Tolkien, J. R. R. (1983) ed. Christopher Tolkien, *The Book of Lost Tales Part I*. London: George Allen & Unwin.

Tolkien, J. R. R. (1984) ed. Christopher Tolkien, *The Book of Lost Tales Part II*. London: George Allen & Unwin.

Tolkien, J. R. R. (1985) ed. Christopher Tolkien, *The Lays of Beleriand*. London: George Allen & Unwin.